You have waited for your king from the King,
but are you prepared to receive him?

This Journal Belongs To:

Date:

PREPARING
FOR YOUR KING
from the

Barbara Nelson Bennett

New Being Books

Lauderhill, FL

The advice and guidance provided in this book are based on the author's personal experience and biblical principles. They are not intended to replace professional counseling or pastoral advice. Always seek God and trusted spiritual leaders when making decisions concerning your life and faith.

Scripture quotations are from the Holy Bible, New Living Translation ® (NLT®). Copyright © 1973, 1978, 1984, 2011 by Biblica, Inc.® Used by permission. All rights reserved worldwide.

Learn more about the author at:
https://barbaranbennett.com

Cover design by Gabyriella Foster

Edited by Annette Purkiss, Allwrite Publishing

ISBN: 979-8-9918479-0-2

Library of Congress Control Number: 2024951021

Cover design by Gabyriella Foster

Printed in the United States of America

AUTHOR'S NOTE

Thank you for joining me on this journey. "Preparing for Your King from the King" is not just a book—it is a heartfelt offering of wisdom, encouragement, and reflection for every woman who desires to prepare herself as a godly wife. I wrote this book with the understanding that marriage is a divine covenant, and that the preparation for such a sacred union goes beyond finding the "right person." It's about becoming the person God has called you to be.

In my own life, I have learned that preparing for marriage is not merely about knowing how to cook, manage a home, or meet society's expectations of a wife. It's about preparing your heart, mind, and spirit to align with God's design for love, submission, compromise, and grace. It's about cultivating a deep, intimate relationship with the Lord, which ultimately shapes how you will love and honor your husband.

This book follows in the footsteps of my previous work, *Waiting for Your King from the King*, where we explored the beauty of singleness and the patience required to wait on God's timing. Now, we turn to the next step—how to prepare yourself for the role of wife with intention, wisdom, and faith. As you go through these pages, you will find reflections, prayers, and practical advice that I hope will encourage you, challenge you, and equip you to be a wife who not only blesses her husband but brings glory to God.

The lessons in this book are not about perfection but about transformation—about allowing God to work on your heart so that you can walk confidently into marriage with a heart rooted in love and humility. Whether you're engaged, dating, or single with marriage on the horizon, my prayer is that this book will lead you closer to God and help you see marriage through His eyes.

As you prepare for your future husband, remember to always keep your eyes fixed on the One who knows you thoroughly, loves you unconditionally, and has already prepared the perfect plan for your life. He is your first King, and your identity in Him is where your true strength lies.

Barbara

CONTENTS

ACKNOWLEDGMENTS

To my husband, Delroy Bennett—my rock. Thank you for being the man God has called you to be. You are truly my king from the King, and I am blessed to walk this journey with you.

To my sister, Audrey Nelson Campbell—thank you for always pushing me toward my greater purpose and standing by my side. Your support and encouragement mean the world to me. I couldn't ask for a better sister.

To my mother, Dorothy M. Nelson—your sacrifices and hard work have not gone unnoticed. Your labor has not been in vain, and you are deeply blessed. I love and honor you for all you've done and for the beautiful person you are.

To my son, Daner B. Hargrove—God has a plan for your life, one filled with hope, purpose, and promise. You are a blessing, a precious gift, and deeply loved. Never forget that.

To Bishop Rohan Diedrick, my mentor who led me to Christ, baptized me and taught me how to have faith.

To Joan Quinland, my best friend and the person who witnessed to me, leading me to Christ.

To Dr. Michelle Phillips for pushing me to the limit and believing in me.

And finally to Claudine Mighty for helping me proof read this book.

BEFORE WE BEGIN...

As women of faith, many of us long for the day we will join in holy matrimony with the husband God has chosen for us. However, before we meet our earthly king, we are called to prepare ourselves by growing closer to our Heavenly King—Jesus Christ. "Preparing for Your King from the King" is a journal designed to guide you through a spiritual journey of self-reflection, growth, and preparation, as God molds your heart and character for the role of a godly wife.

This journal is divided into several key sections, each aimed at preparing you for marriage through biblical principles and personal reflection:

1. Becoming the Bride of Christ
Before we become a wife to our earthly husband, we must first understand what it means to be the bride of Christ. In this section, you will explore how your relationship with Jesus lays the foundation for all other relationships, teaching you to trust, love, and serve from a place of divine connection.

2. Cultivating a Servant's Heart
Marriage is a covenant that requires selflessness and a servant's heart. This section will help you focus on developing a heart of service—not only in preparation for your future husband but also for the people around you. Learning to serve as Christ served helps us mirror the love and humility needed in marriage.

3. Trusting God's Timing
Waiting for the right person can be challenging, but trusting God's perfect timing is crucial. In this section, you will reflect on the importance of patience and faith as you wait for God to align your path with your future husband. You'll be encouraged to lean on His promises rather than rushing ahead in your own strength.

4. Conflict Resolution & the Power of Submission in Marriage
No relationship is without conflict, but learning how to resolve issues in a way that honors God is key to a strong and lasting marriage. This section focuses on the biblical understanding of submission and partnership, exploring how both men and women are called to submit to one another in love, and how to handle disagreements with grace and respect.

BEFORE WE BEGIN...

5. Becoming a Wife Prepared by the King

This final section is all about embracing your God-given identity and the qualities that make you the wife your future husband will need. As you prepare, you'll reflect on how God is shaping you to be a partner, a nurturer, and a spiritual support in your future marriage.

Throughout this journal, you'll find opportunities for prayer, personal reflection, and practical applications to help you on your journey. Use this time to allow God to speak to your heart, shape your spirit, and prepare your life for the incredible blessing of marriage. Trust that as you seek Him first, He will equip you to be the wife He has designed you to be with a husband specially called by Him.

Let this be your season of preparation, trusting in the King as you prepare for your king.

BECOMING THE BRIDE OF CHRIST

Before we can step into the role of a godly wife, we must first understand our identity as the bride of Christ. This concept is foundational because it speaks to the core of who we are—daughters of the Most High, chosen and set apart to be loved deeply by Him. Without this understanding, we risk approaching marriage as a means to fill a void only Christ was meant to satisfy. Before you prepare for your earthly king, you must first embrace the truth that you are the bride of the King of kings.

In today's world, many of us define ourselves by our relationships, achievements, or even our shortcomings. We look for validation and love from the people around us, hoping that they will see us, cherish us, and complete us. However, the truth is, no human can complete what God began in us. Our worth and identity cannot be anchored in a spouse, no matter how wonderful or Godly he is. Our first and truest identity is found in being the bride of Christ.

Revelation 19:7-8 "Let us rejoice and be glad and give Him glory! For the wedding of the Lamb has come, and His bride has made herself ready. Fine linen, bright and clean, was given her to wear."

The imagery here is powerful. The bride (the Church, and by extension, each of us) is made ready—purified and clothed in righteousness. This isn't a surface-level righteousness that comes from simply doing the "right" things; it's a deep, transformational righteousness that comes from the cleansing work of Christ in our lives. On our own, we can never be righteous. It is the blood of Jesus Christ who died on the cross that cleanses us and makes us clean. Through faith in Jesus Christ, we are made whole and we are cleansed by His blood.

Isaiah 1:18 "Come now, let's settle this," says the Lord. Though your sins are like scarlet, I will make them as white as snow. Though they are red like crimson, I will make them as white as wool."

Isaiah 64:6 "We are all infected and impure with sin. When we display our righteous deeds, they are nothing but filthy rags. Like autumn leaves, we wither and fall, and our sins sweep us away like the wind"

So, before we prepare for marriage, we must ask ourselves: Have we allowed Christ to prepare us as His bride? Have we embraced His love fully or are we still looking for someone else to fulfill what only He can? When we understand our identity as His bride, we can enter into marriage with a whole heart—one that is not looking for completion, but rather for partnership.

Have you heard of the term, "God-shaped hole?" This is referring to the area in everyone's lives that can really only be filled by God. More often than not, people will try to fill that hole with other things besides God such as: career, money, drugs, and even relationships. However, if we continue to do this, then the hole will never be satisfied. Think about it like this: Do you remember your kids playing with those shape puzzles when they were just toddlers? There was a hole for the circle, the square, and the triangle and three corresponding blocks. Your child might have tried putting the square block into the circle hole and found that it did not fit and ended up getting frustrated, throwing the block across the room. Just like the square block cannot fit in the circle hole, things and people cannot satisfy you and fill that void that only God can fill. When people try to fill that hole with anything else besides God, they often get frustrated, just like a toddler and will point the finger at or blame everything and everyone else, including God, for feeling unfulfilled.

This is just like Solomon, who was a man of great wisdom. Although he had many wives and was rich, Solomon still felt a void. This can be seen throughout the book of Ecclesiastes. Solomon tried everything under the sun to fill that void, but he ultimately came to the conclusion that God is the only one who could satisfy him. Everything else was "vanity," or simply meaningless, as he stated.

When you come to this conclusion just like Solomon had, then you will stop expecting your future spouse to fill that void and complete you. You will just be looking for a companion or partner in life who may be imperfect, but can help you build and continue to lead you as God intended.

REFLECT

What does it mean to you personally to be the bride of Christ? Take time to meditate on this identity. How does viewing yourself as His bride change the way you see yourself, your value, and your future?

_____

_____

_____

_____

_____

_____

_____

_____

_____

_____

_____

_____

_____

REFLECT

How have relationships (past or present) affected your view of your identity? Have you allowed rejection, betrayal, or approval from others to define who you are? In what ways might you be seeking validation outside of your relationship with Christ?

_____

_____

_____

_____

_____

_____

_____

_____

_____

_____

_____

_____

Healing from Brokenness

For many women, the journey to becoming the bride of Christ involves healing. We all carry wounds—whether from past relationships, family dynamics, or the lies we've believed about ourselves. Sometimes, we come into this season of preparation with the weight of past mistakes or the shame of brokenness that we don't know how to shake.

Here's the beautiful truth: Christ doesn't just call you His bride; He redeems you as His bride. He takes your scars, your brokenness, and your regrets and transforms them into something beautiful. His healing allows us to fully receive His love, redemption, and purpose without the hindrances of past wounds. When we carry unresolved pain or brokenness, it can create barriers to trusting and fully submitting to Christ. Healing restores us, making us whole and able to engage in a relationship with Him from a place of strength, peace, and joy. It ultimately helps prepare us for our earthly mate, so we can move forward in a relationship without pain, shame, guilt or fear.

Isaiah 61:3 speaks directly to this transformation: "beauty for ashes, the oil of joy for mourning, and a garment of praise for the spirit of heaviness." This verse reminds us that God doesn't just heal us; He exchanges our sorrow and brokenness for joy and beauty. He redeems the parts of our lives that felt shattered and heavy, allowing us to wear His righteousness and praise. This healing is what enables us to step into our role as Christ's bride, with renewed strength and a spirit of worship, prepared to walk in the fullness of our relationship with Him.

Isaiah 61:3 "beauty for ashes, the oil of joy for mourning, and a garment of praise for the spirit of heaviness"

No matter what you have been through—whether it's heartbreak, disappointment or sin—Jesus is able and willing to heal you. But you must come to Him first. Before you can give yourself to another person, allow Jesus to make you whole. Your future marriage will be a reflection of the love and healing you've received from Christ. The more you allow Him to restore and renew you, the more you will be able to love your future husband from a place of wholeness rather than neediness.

REFLECT

Where do you see patterns of self-protection or fear manifesting in your relationships? Do you find yourself building walls or keeping people at a distance to avoid being hurt again? What would it look like to trust God to protect your heart while remaining open to others?

_____

_____

_____

_____

_____

_____

_____

_____

_____

_____

_____

_____

REFLECT

How have your past hurts shaped your expectations for future relationships, especially marriage? Are you expecting your future husband to "fix" or "heal" parts of you that only God can heal? How can you invite God into those areas before marriage?

_____

_____

_____

_____

_____

_____

_____

_____

_____

_____

_____

Surrendering Control

Being the bride of Christ also means learning to surrender control. As women, we often desire security and stability, especially when it comes to our future. We may have dreams of what our marriage will look like, the kind of husband we want, and the timeline we hope to follow. But God's plans for us often look different than what we imagine. **Proverbs 3:5-6 reminds us to "Trust in the Lord with all your heart and lean not on your own understanding; in all your ways submit to Him, and He will make your paths straight."** This includes the path to marriage.

Jeremiah 29:11 " For I know the plans I have for you," says the Lord. "They are plans for good and not for disaster, to give you a future and a hope."

Surrendering control doesn't mean that we stop desiring a husband or planning for the future. Instead, it means that we submit those desires to God, trusting that He knows what is best for us. It means that we stop trying to force relationships that aren't God's best, and we wait patiently for His timing. It means that we allow God to write our love story, trusting that His plans are far better than our own. Surrendering control also involves letting go of the fear of being "too late" or missing out on God's plan. Sometimes, the waiting season feels endless, and it's easy to wonder if God has forgotten us or if we've somehow missed our opportunity. But remember, God is never late. He is always on time. **Ecclesiastes 3:11 says, "He has made everything beautiful in its time."** This includes your marriage. You don't need to strive or stress—your King has it all under control.

REFLECT

In what areas of your life do you still struggle with surrendering control to God? How can you invite Him into those spaces as you prepare for a future relationship? How can you shift your mindset to seeing love as a form of worship and service to God, trusting that He will guide you in loving your future spouse?

REFLECT

Are there people or situations in your life where you struggle to surrender control and trust God to help you extend love, grace, or forgiveness? How might God be using these moments to teach you about releasing control and trusting Him to guide your love for your future spouse? What is God showing you about surrendering to His way of loving others?

Loving Like Christ

Being the bride of Christ means we are called to love like Christ. This is the kind of love that marriage requires—sacrificial, unconditional, and patient. But we cannot love our future husband with Christ-like love unless we first receive that love from Christ Himself. It's in our relationship with Him that we learn what true love looks like. It's in experiencing His grace, mercy, and forgiveness that we are equipped to offer those same things in marriage.

Ephesians 5:1-2 "Follow God's example, therefore, as dearly loved children and walk in the way of love, just as Christ loved us and gave Himself up for us as a fragrant offering and sacrifice to God."

This is why our relationship with Christ must come first. We are called to love our spouses as Christ loves the Church, but if we haven't first experienced that love from Jesus, we will constantly be seeking it from our spouse. Marriage is not about two people completing each other; it's about two people who are already complete in Christ, coming together to reflect His love to the world.

Jesus showed immense, unconditional love. His love for us is what made Him sacrifice His life for our salvation. Jesus even loved those who hated Him. In fact, His love is beyond our human comprehension, but we should strive everyday to conform our ways and thoughts to His likeness, seeking the Spirit for guidance and direction in this regard. One of the clearest examples of Jesus' unconditional love is found in John 8:1-11, the story of the woman caught in adultery. Religious leaders brought a woman before Jesus, demanding that she be stoned according to the law. Instead of condemning her, Jesus responded with grace, saying, *"Let him who is without sin cast the first stone."* One by one, the accusers left, and Jesus turned to the woman and said, *"Neither do I condemn you. Go and sin no more."* Jesus did not excuse sin, but He also did not withhold mercy. He offered forgiveness without conditions, demonstrating that His love is not based on perfection but on grace and redemption. Jesus' unconditional love reflects how we are called to love our partners—with **grace**, **forgiveness**, and a **commitment** to growth rather than condemnation. Let's be honest, there are going to be days when our future spouse is going to upset, annoy, or make decisions that anger us. Still, that does not mean we should withhold love. We are to love them beyond their imperfections, like Jesus loves us.

REFLECT

Reflect on a time when someone showed you sacrificial love. How did that impact you, and how can you carry that example into your future marriage? How does Christ's sacrifice shape your understanding of love?

_____

_____

_____

_____

_____

_____

_____

_____

_____

_____

_____

REFLECT

Love often requires self-sacrifice. Reflect on moments when loving someone required you to go beyond your comfort zone. How can these experiences prepare you for the sacrifices that come with marriage?

_____

_____

_____

_____

_____

_____

_____

_____

_____

_____

_____

_____

REFLECT

Christ's love was marked by humility. He lowered Himself to serve others, even washing His disciples' feet. In what areas of your life do you need to embrace humility in order to love others better? How can you practice humility in your future marriage?

_____

_____

_____

_____

_____

_____

_____

_____

_____

_____

_____

_____

Preparation Prayer

Father, I thank You that I am first and foremost Your bride. Help me to understand the depth of Your love for me and to find my worth in You alone. Heal the broken areas of my heart, and help me to surrender control of my future to You. Teach me to love like You love, so that when You bring my future husband into my life, I will be ready to love him with a heart that is full of You.
Amen

Work Out Your Faith:

Write a Letter of Encouragement

Activity: Write a letter to someone in your life (a friend, family member, or church leader) who may need encouragement. Express how much they mean to you, how you appreciate their presence in your life, and any positive traits they may not see in themselves.

Purpose: Encouragement is a form of service. In marriage, you'll often need to lift up your spouse during difficult times. Practicing now will help you develop a heart that naturally speaks life and support into others.

CULTIVATING A SERVANT'S HEART

One of the most vital aspects of preparing to be a godly wife is learning to cultivate a servant's heart. Jesus Himself modeled this type of heart throughout His ministry. He was never too proud to serve, never too busy to put the needs of others before His own. As the bride of Christ, and as future wives, we are called to embody that same selflessness and humility.

The world often teaches us that love is about what we receive: affection, attention, validation. But the love of Christ flips that on its head. It shows us that true love is found in what we give. When we serve others, especially our spouse, we reflect the very heart of Jesus.

Christ's Example of Service

One of the most profound examples of Christ's servant heart is found in John 13, where He washes His disciples' feet:

"He poured water into a basin and began to wash the disciples' feet, drying them with the towel that was wrapped around Him... 'Now that I, your Lord and Teacher, have washed your feet, you also should wash one another's feet. I have set you an example that you should do as I have done for you.'" (John 13:5, 14-15)

Jesus, the Son of God, the King of kings, humbled Himself to the lowest form of service—washing the feet of His followers. This wasn't a symbolic gesture. In that time, washing feet was the work of the lowest servants, because people walked in dirt, mud, and filth. Yet, Jesus, in His perfect humility, did it as an act of love. His actions remind us that love is not above serving in the most ordinary, mundane, or difficult ways.

As you prepare for marriage, ask yourself: Are you willing to serve your future husband in the way Christ served His disciples? Are you willing to put his needs before your own, not in a way that diminishes your value, but in a way that exalts Christ's love through your actions? This doesn't mean losing yourself or being a doormat. It means approaching marriage with the mindset of Christ—who, though He was God, humbled Himself to the point of service.

REFLECT

Reflect on moments when you've chosen humility over pride. Where in your relationships have you had to humble yourself, and how did that shape the way you served others? Are there areas in your life where you still struggle with pride, especially when it comes to serving?

_____

_____

_____

_____

_____

_____

_____

_____

_____

_____

_____

_____

REFLECT

It's important to remember that serving others doesn't mean neglecting your own needs. How can you practice Christ-like service while still maintaining a healthy balance of self-care?

_____

_____

_____

_____

_____

_____

_____

_____

_____

_____

_____

_____

Serving in Marriage

When we think about marriage, we often imagine grand gestures of love—flowers, date nights, romantic vacations. However, true service in marriage is found in the daily, often unseen moments. It's in the way you support your husband after a long day, listen to his struggles, and encourage him in his walk with God. It's in the times when you choose to hold your tongue instead of speaking words out of frustration, or when you forgive even when you don't feel like it.

Serving in marriage is about meeting the needs of your spouse, even when it costs you something. It's about putting their well-being above your own comfort or desires. And as you practice this kind of love, you will find that it transforms your heart. Serving is not just about what you give; it's about what God is doing in you as you give.

Ephesians 5:21 "Submit to one another out of reverence for Christ."

Balance of Service and Partnership

While it's essential to have a servant's heart, marriage is not one-sided. It's a partnership, and both husband and wife are called to serve one another. Ephesians 5:21 says, "Submit to one another out of reverence for Christ." This mutual submission, as further described in Ephesians 5:22-33, is key to a healthy, God-honoring marriage, reflecting the love and respect spouses should have for one another. Thus, serving each other within the marriage is a form of honoring Christ and fulfilling His purpose for the relationship.

You are not just preparing to serve your husband; you are preparing to walk alongside him as a partner, supporting him as he serves you too. God designed marriage to be a reflection of Christ's love for the Church, a love that gives and receives, that sacrifices and honors both individuals.

In marriage, you will have seasons where your spouse may be the one who needs more support, and seasons where you are the one who needs to lean on him. That's the beauty of partnership. A godly marriage requires both husband and wife to pour into each other, continually reflecting Christ's love through acts of service, kindness, and mutual respect.

REFLECT

Often, we can feel that serving others diminishes our value, but Jesus teaches us that serving actually brings us closer to Him. How can you shift your mindset to see service as a strength, and not a burden? In what ways has your relationship with Christ empowered you to serve more freely?

REFLECT

Be honest about any concerns you may have regarding service in marriage. Are you afraid of losing your independence, being taken for granted, or being in a one-sided relationship? How can you trust God to provide balance and mutual love in your future marriage?

_____

_____

_____

_____

_____

_____

_____

_____

_____

_____

_____

_____

Honoring Our Bodies

In preparing for your future spouse, it's important to honor and care for your body as it is not just yours, but also a temple of the Holy Spirit. The Bible says in 1 Corinthians 6:19-20: "Do you not know that your bodies are temples of the Holy Spirit, who is in you, whom you have received from God? You are not your own; you were bought at a price. Therefore honor God with your bodies."

This passage emphasizes that our bodies are sacred spaces where God's Spirit resides. As we prepare for marriage, treating our bodies with respect, nurturing them with health and care, and exercising self-discipline are all acts of servanthood to God. By doing so, we are aligning ourselves with His will and cultivating a heart of service that mirrors the love and care we are called to show in a future marriage.

Moreover, taking care of your body reflects the commitment to honor God and others, particularly your future spouse, with purity and devotion. Just as you prepare your heart to serve God, preparing your body involves living in a way that reflects His goodness, self-control, and grace. When we cultivate servanthood to the Spirit of God in this way, we embody the love and faithfulness He calls us to in every aspect of our lives.

1 Corinthians 6:19-20 "Do you not know that your bodies are temples of the Holy Spirit, who is in you, whom you have received from God? You are not your own; you were bought at a price. Therefore honor God with your bodies."

When we neglect this principle—whether through unhealthy habits, impurity, or lack of self-control—it can lead to broken trust, insecurity, and emotional barriers in marriage. We may also struggle with the emotional, spiritual, and physical health needed to foster intimacy and trust with a future spouse:

- **Physical Consequences**: Can lead to physical issues that may affect intimacy and overall well-being in marriage.
- **Emotional Consequences**: Can lower self-esteem, making it harder to feel secure and valued in a marriage.
- **Spiritual Consequences**: We distance ourselves from God, which can strain our ability to love and serve our spouse as God intended.

REFLECT

How do you currently view your body in relation to your spiritual walk with God? Are there areas where you struggle to honor your body as a temple of the Holy Spirit? How has this affected you personally (e.g. health, self-worth) and your past relationships?

_____

_____

_____

_____

_____

_____

_____

_____

_____

_____

_____

_____

REFLECT

What steps can you take to improve your emotional, spiritual, and physical well-being in preparation for a healthy, intimate relationship? In what ways have past experiences (emotional or physical) affected your ability to trust others? How can surrendering these struggles to God help restore your heart for future intimacy?

_____

_____

_____

_____

_____

_____

_____

_____

_____

_____

_____

_____

Preparation Prayer

Lord, help me to have a heart that mirrors Yours—a heart that serves, loves, and gives without seeking anything in return. Teach me how to walk in humility and selflessness, just as You did when You washed Your disciples' feet. As I prepare for marriage, show me how to serve my future husband with grace and joy, and help me to always see service as an act of worship unto You.

Amen

Work Out Your Faith:

Write a Letter of Encouragement

Activity: Choose someone in your community who is struggling—maybe a single parent, someone who is sick, or a family facing hardship—and prepare a meal for them. This simple act of service allows you to offer practical help and show Christ's love in action.

Purpose: To practice Christ-like compassion in a tangible way. This simple act reflects the heart of servanthood by meeting a basic need —nourishment—while demonstrating love and care for others. Jesus often met physical needs before addressing spiritual ones, and this activity allows you to follow His example by reaching out to someone who may be struggling or overwhelmed.

TRUSTING GOD'S TIMING

The Bible gives us many beautiful examples of what it looks like to wait on God's timing in relationships. Two of the most powerful stories of patience, faith, and trust in God's sovereign plan are those of Ruth and Boaz and Rachel and Jacob. These stories, found in the Old Testament, aren't just about romance; they're about divine alignment, the beauty of God's provision, and how He orchestrates every step of our lives—even in the most personal areas, such as marriage.

Ruth and Boaz: A Story of Divine Alignment

The story of Ruth and Boaz begins with loss and uncertainty. Ruth, a foreigner and a widow, found herself in a foreign land with no husband and no means to provide for herself or her mother-in-law, Naomi. Yet, Ruth made a bold and faith-filled decision: instead of returning to her homeland and people, she chose to follow Naomi back to Bethlehem, declaring that Naomi's God would be her God.

Ruth's decision to follow Naomi and serve her reflected a deep trust in God's provision. She didn't know what her future held, but she knew that faithfulness and obedience would lead her exactly where she needed to be. In **Ruth 2:12**, Boaz says to her, **"May the Lord repay you for what you have done. May you be richly rewarded by the Lord, the God of Israel, under whose wings you have come to take refuge."** Ruth's humble, quiet faith brought her under the covering of God's care.

Boaz was a man of standing and godly character, a distant relative of Naomi's deceased husband. When Ruth went to glean in his fields, Boaz noticed her, but not for superficial reasons. He saw her kindness, her devotion, her hard work, and her faith in God. Ruth didn't have to strive or seek attention—Boaz was drawn to her because of her inner beauty, her heart that radiated Christ-like love, and her integrity. This is a profound message to us today: when you focus on your relationship with God and faithfully walk in obedience, God will place you where you are meant to be—just as He placed Ruth in the path of Boaz.

Boaz's role in Ruth's life is significant because he acts as her kinsman-redeemer, a role that foreshadows Christ. Just as Boaz redeemed Ruth and restored her position in society, so Christ redeems us, bringing restoration and new beginnings. The love between Ruth and Boaz wasn't rushed or based on fleeting emotions; it was built on a foundation of respect, integrity, and God's timing. Boaz didn't take advantage of Ruth's vulnerability as a widow, but instead protected her, honored her, and eventually married her, fulfilling God's plan for both their lives.

In your own journey, the story of Ruth and Boaz reminds you to trust in God's timing and provision. Instead of focusing on finding the "right person," focus on being the person God has called you to be. Just as Ruth was faithful in her everyday tasks, trust that as you are faithful to God in your singleness, He is preparing and aligning things behind the scenes in ways you cannot yet see. Boaz came at just the right time in Ruth's life—not too early and not too late—because God's timing is always perfect.

Rachel and Jacob: A Lesson in Endurance and Sacrificial Love

The story of Jacob and Rachel, found in Genesis 29, offers a profound example of patience, endurance, and the willingness to sacrifice in the name of love. Unlike most love stories, theirs was marked by challenges, deception, and a long period of waiting. Yet, it is also a testimony to the strength of Jacob's love for Rachel and his unwavering commitment to her. Through their journey, we learn about trusting in God's timing, remaining faithful in adversity, and the refining power of waiting.

Jacob first encountered Rachel when he arrived in Haran, fleeing from his brother Esau's wrath after deceiving him for the birthright blessing. Weary from his travels, Jacob saw Rachel, the daughter of his uncle Laban, and was immediately struck by her beauty. This love-at-first-sight moment is significant because it marks the beginning of one of the Bible's longest periods of waiting for marriage. The instant attraction Jacob felt for Rachel sparked a deep commitment in him, but that commitment would be tested for years to come.

Jacob approached Laban with a bold offer: he would work for seven years to marry Rachel. The Bible tells us that Jacob loved Rachel so much that "the seven years seemed like only a few days to him because of his love for her" (Genesis 29:20). This verse is a beautiful illustration of how love, when pure and true, transforms even the most difficult tasks and long waits into something bearable, even joyful. Jacob's love for Rachel made his years of labor seem light, and he willingly took on this challenge because he knew she was worth the wait.

However, after completing his seven years of work, Jacob faced an unexpected and heartbreaking obstacle. On his wedding night, Laban deceived him by substituting his older daughter Leah in place of Rachel. Jacob woke up the next morning to realize that he had been tricked into marrying Leah. Naturally, Jacob was devastated and angry, but instead of lashing out or abandoning his pursuit of Rachel, he chose to persevere. Laban agreed to give Rachel to Jacob in exchange for another seven years of labor.

Jacob's second seven-year period of working for Rachel reveals much about the nature of godly love and sacrifice. He didn't grumble, manipulate the situation, or try to find a shortcut to get what he wanted. Jacob's love for Rachel motivated him to honor the commitment he had made, even though it meant enduring additional hardship. This speaks to the kind of love that goes beyond feelings and convenience —it's a love rooted in selflessness and dedication, one that mirrors the love Christ has for His bride, the Church.

Divine Lessons in Love

- **Focus on Your Own Growth**: Ruth focused on her relationship with God and her faithfulness to Naomi before Boaz even noticed her. Rachel's story reminds us that even when things are delayed or complicated, God is still preparing the right situation. Use this time to grow in godliness, character, and wisdom, knowing that this season is not about finding someone, but about becoming who God has called you to be.

- **Trust God's Timing Completely**: God's plan is always better than our own. You may feel anxious or uncertain, wondering when your husband will come, but God's timing is perfect. Just as He brought Boaz into Ruth's life at the right time and allowed Jacob and Rachel's love to grow through years of waiting, He will bring the right person into your life in His divine time. Don't rush the process—God is working even when you can't see it.

' **Esteem Sacrificial Love**: Jacob's story is also a powerful example of sacrificial love. He didn't just wait for Rachel—he worked for her. He toiled in the fields, endured hardship and faced deception, all because he loved her deeply. Jacob's willingness to sacrifice his time and energy reflects the kind of love we should seek in a marriage—a love that is willing to sacrifice for the other person. This kind of love mirrors the sacrificial love of Christ. Jesus gave Himself up for us, not because it was easy, but because His love for us was greater than the cost. In the same way, a godly marriage requires a level of sacrifice. It's not always going to be easy or convenient, but when love is rooted in Christ, it has the power to endure hardship, just as Jacob's love for Rachel endured through years of waiting and labor.

Contrasting Ruth and Rachel: Two Journeys of Trust

Both Ruth and Rachel exemplify patience and trust in different ways. Ruth's story is marked by a quiet surrender to God's plan without knowing what her future held. Rachel's story, on the other hand, is one of longing and anticipation, where she knew who she wanted to be with, but the journey to get there was long and fraught with obstacles. Both women trusted God's timing, though their experiences were very different.

- Ruth trusted God even when she didn't know if marriage would ever be a part of her future. Her faithfulness in the everyday led her to Boaz, her redeemer, and ultimately into the lineage of Christ.

- Rachel, on the other hand, waited for years, watching Jacob work for her, and enduring family complications along the way. Her story reminds us that even when we know who or what we are waiting for, the journey can still be long, but it is always worth it when we trust God's plan.

Both stories teach us the value of trust, patience, and faith in God's timing. Whether we are in a season of uncertainty, like Ruth, or in a season of waiting for something we already long for, like Rachel, the key is to keep our eyes on God and trust that He is leading us toward the good He has prepared for us.

REFLECT

Reflect on moments where you've felt impatience or frustration in waiting for your spouse. How can you shift your focus to trusting God's timing rather than your own? What is the most challenging part about waiting on God?

_____

_____

_____

_____

_____

_____

_____

_____

_____

_____

_____

REFLECT

Rachel had to wait and watch as Leah married Jacob first. How do you respond when others seem to receive what you're praying and waiting for? What steps can you take to guard your heart against jealousy, resentment, or discouragement while waiting for your own prayers to be answered?

REFLECT

God had a greater plan for Jacob and Rachel, even though their path wasn't easy. How does this encourage you to trust that God has a greater plan for your relationships and your future? In what ways can you surrender your plans and desires to God's greater purpose, even if it means enduring unexpected hardships or delays?

_____

_____

_____

_____

_____

_____

_____

_____

_____

_____

_____

_____

REFLECT

In what ways can you model Christ's love by being faithful, enduring, and committed in your relationships, even when they require significant sacrifice? What sacrifices do you feel are or have been the greatest challenges for you in preparing for your spouse?

_____

_____

_____

_____

_____

_____

_____

_____

_____

_____

_____

REFLECT

In your relationships, do you feel that the sacrifices you make are met with reciprocal efforts? Should relationship sacrifices always be balanced, or are there times when one person may need to give more? How can you approach these situations with grace and understanding?

_____

_____

_____

_____

_____

_____

_____

_____

_____

_____

_____

Preparation Prayer

Heavenly Father, I come before You, recognizing that Your timing is perfect, even when it's hard to understand. Just as Jacob waited patiently for Rachel, help me to trust in Your plans for my life, even when I can't see the full picture.

Lord, I pray for a heart that rests in You during my waiting seasons. Give me the patience to endure without losing hope, and the wisdom to understand that waiting is not passive, but an active part of Your process of shaping me. Teach me to be like Jacob, who worked faithfully, trusting that what You had promised would come to pass. Help me to love sacrificially, as Jacob did, and to trust in the unseen ways You are working behind the scenes for my good.

Father, I release my desires and timelines into Your hands. Mold my character, refine my faith, and help me to grow in the fruits of the Spirit, especially patience and love. Prepare my heart to be a godly spouse, and teach me to love like Christ—selflessly, enduringly, and faithfully. I pray that in my waiting, I will grow closer to You and become more like the person You have called me to be.

In Jesus' name, Amen.

PREPARING WITH PURPOSE

In the journey of waiting for your future spouse, it's important to recognize that this time is not wasted. It's a season of development—spiritually, emotionally, and relationally. Like a seed planted in the soil, there is much growth happening beneath the surface even when you can't see it. God is using this time to mold you into the woman He has called you to be, preparing you for the role of a godly wife.

Importance of Becoming Before Receiving

It's important to focus on personal growth and wholeness before entering a relationship because doing so leads to healthier, more fulfilling connections and helps in recognizing potential red flags or incompatibilities. One of the greatest misconceptions is that we need to focus only on finding "the one" or waiting passively for our future spouse to arrive. However, God's design for relationships isn't about just waiting—it's about becoming. He is far more interested in *who you are* becoming in Christ than in simply giving you *what you desire*.

Just as Boaz recognized Ruth's character long before any romantic interest blossomed, the kind of woman you are becoming now is what will prepare you for a thriving, God-honoring marriage. Ruth was known for her integrity, hard work, and faithfulness to her mother-in-law, Naomi, before Boaz ever noticed her as a potential wife. She was committed to doing what was right, regardless of the circumstances. Her character shone in a way that caught Boaz's attention because it reflected God's heart. Your character likewise speaks louder than anything else. Similarly, Jacob didn't just passively wait for Rachel. He worked tirelessly, motivated by his deep love for her along with his sense of responsibility and purpose. His years of labor weren't just about earning her hand in marriage; they were about proving his commitment, perseverance, and strength of character.

Instead of solely seeking certain qualities in a partner, we should cultivate those same attributes within ourselves. For example, if we pray for a spouse who is physically fit and health-conscious, yet we neglect our own diet and exercise, we are not aligning our actions with our desires. True preparation for a relationship involves developing the character, habits, and lifestyle that we seek in another person. This concept is explored in depth in the journal "**Waiting for Your King from the King**," which guides readers on personal growth journey.

REFLECT

What are some of your best *nonphysical* characteristics? How can they enhance your relationship with your future spouse? How are you actively addressing aspects of your character that may have hindered your ability to build and maintain healthy relationships?

_____

_____

_____

_____

_____

_____

_____

_____

_____

_____

_____

_____

REFLECT

Are you focusing on developing a gentle spirit, compassion for others, and integrity in all you do? Why or why not? How do you believe the process of personal growth and self-discovery before meeting your spouse will influence the foundation of your marriage? In what ways can you actively work on becoming the best version of yourself in preparation for this lifelong commitment?

Being a Woman of Virtue

Being a "woman of virtue" means cultivating godly character, integrity, and wisdom while living in alignment with biblical principles. A woman of virtue seeks to honor God first in her heart, mind, and actions, which in turn prepares her to be the kind of wife who reflects Christ's love and grace in marriage and other significant relationships. The Bible provides a beautiful illustration of this in Proverbs 31:10-31, which describes the qualities of a virtuous woman. Here are some key characteristics of a woman of virtue in preparation for marriage:

1. **God-Centered Character**: A virtuous woman fears the Lord above all. Proverbs 31:30 says, *"Charm is deceptive, and beauty is fleeting; but a woman who fears the Lord is to be praised."* Her strength and dignity come from her relationship with God, not just from external qualities.

2. **Wisdom and Prudence**: She is wise and discerning. Proverbs 31:26 highlights that *"She speaks with wisdom, and faithful instruction is on her tongue."* This wisdom comes from her intimacy with God, and it guides her decisions and actions in life and relationships.

3. **Hardworking and Diligent**: She works diligently and uses her gifts to bless others, as seen in Proverbs 31:13-19, which describes her industriousness in providing for her household. She prepares for her future by being responsible, resourceful, and disciplined.

4. **Kind and Compassionate**: She is compassionate and generous, extending love to others. Proverbs 31:20 says, *"She opens her arms to the poor and extends her hands to the needy."* In preparing for a marriage, cultivating a heart that serves others helps foster empathy, patience, and humility in relationships.

5. **Trustworthy and Faithful**: She is trustworthy, and her future husband will have full confidence in her. Proverbs 31:11 says, *"Her husband has full confidence in her and lacks nothing of value."* This faithfulness extends not only to her future spouse but also to her relationship with God.

6. **Inner Strength and Dignity**: Virtue includes strength and dignity, qualities that allow a woman to face challenges with grace and courage. Proverbs 31:25 states, *"She is clothed with strength and dignity; she can laugh at the days to come."* This inner fortitude comes from trusting in God's plan and timing, including for marriage.

REFLECT

What does it mean to be a "woman of virtue" in today's world? How can you intentionally pursue this standard?

_____

_____

_____

_____

_____

_____

_____

_____

_____

_____

_____

_____

REFLECT

What steps can you take to ensure your values reflect God's will and desire for your life as you prepare for marriage? In what ways can pursuing God's wisdom and love help you grow as a loving, faithful, and supportive spouse? How are you nurturing these qualities now?

_____

_____

_____

_____

_____

_____

_____

_____

_____

_____

_____

_____

CONFLICT RESOLUTION &
THE POWER OF SUBMISSION

Conflict resolution in marriage goes beyond just addressing surface-level disagreements; it is a test of your heart's posture toward your spouse and toward God. Many believe that conflict in marriage means something is fundamentally wrong, but in reality, conflict can be a tool that God uses to refine you both individually and as a couple.

Imagine a couple having a disagreement about finances—a common marital issue. The husband may want to invest in a business venture, while the wife is concerned about the risks. If they both hold tightly to their own opinions without seeking understanding, the conflict will only escalate. However, if they step back and ask, "What is God teaching us through this situation?" the conflict becomes an opportunity for growth.

Instead of seeing your spouse as the opposition, remember that both of you are on the same team, working toward a unified purpose: to glorify God in your marriage. Conflict resolution starts with humility. When you approach a disagreement with a willingness to listen and a heart to understand rather than to be understood, you allow God to work through the tension to bring about deeper unity.

A practical example would be setting aside time after a disagreement to pray together. Laying your concerns before God helps you remember that the issue at hand is temporary, but your relationship and its reflection of Christ's love are eternal. By inviting God into the midst of your conflicts, you shift the focus from proving a point to preserving peace.

Importance of Compromise

Compromise is not about sacrificing your convictions or losing your voice. It's about honoring the partnership God has established. Marriage is not about "who wins," but about both people winning together by finding common ground. Think about compromise as a bridge that connects two people with different needs, perspectives, and preferences.

For instance, say you're planning a vacation, and one of you wants a quiet retreat in the mountains while the other prefers a beach getaway. Without compromise, this situation could easily lead to frustration and resentment. But compromise may look like alternating between locations on different vacations, or finding a spot where you can experience elements of both. In doing so, you're showing that your partner's desires are just as important as your own.

In deeper issues, such as how to raise children or manage career responsibilities, compromise becomes even more essential. It's about creating an environment where both partners feel heard and respected, and where each person is willing to yield for the sake of harmony. **Ephesians 4:2-3** calls us to **"be completely humble and gentle; be patient, bearing with one another in love. Make every effort to keep the unity of the Spirit through the bond of peace."** This unity comes from learning when to compromise, when to speak, and when to simply let go.

Compromise doesn't mean you're giving up; it means you trust that God will fill the gaps where you and your spouse can't seem to meet perfectly. You're choosing unity over personal satisfaction.

REFLECT

When was the last time you experienced conflict in a relationship? Did you prioritize being right or did you seek to honor God and your partner through humility and understanding?

_____

_____

_____

_____

_____

_____

_____

_____

_____

_____

_____

_____

REFLECT

How can you better invite God's presence into the middle of a conflict? What practical steps can you take to ensure that He guides your conversations and emotions?

_____

_____

_____

_____

_____

_____

_____

_____

_____

_____

_____

Biblical Submission: What It Really Means

Submission in marriage has often been misunderstood and misused. However, biblical submission is a beautiful act of trust, rooted in love and mutual respect. The world may see submission as an act of weakness or inferiority, but within a Christian marriage, submission is a reflection of Christ's relationship with the church—a relationship built on unconditional love, sacrifice, and service.

In **Ephesians 5:22-24,** Paul instructs wives to submit to their husbands **"as to the Lord,"** and husbands to love their wives **"as Christ loved the church and gave himself up for her"** (Ephesians 5:25). Submission here is not about dominance or control; it's about order, leadership, and sacrificial love. Just as Christ leads the church, the husband is called to lead the family with humility, wisdom, and deep love.

Submission, in its truest form, is about trust. You are trusting God's design for marriage and trusting your husband to lead you as he follows Christ. When a husband leads with the love of Christ, submission becomes an act of partnership, not oppression.

Imagine a wife who is deeply skilled in finances. Instead of demanding control, she uses her expertise to advise and support her husband as he leads the family in stewardship. She submits not by being silent but by honoring his leadership while actively contributing her gifts and wisdom. In turn, the husband honors her input and cherishes her as a valuable partner.

Submission, then, is not about silence or invisibility; it is about empowering your husband to lead in a way that glorifies God. When both partners are rooted in God's love, submission becomes a beautiful dance of mutual trust, service, and unity.

REFLECT

What does submission mean to you personally? How has your view been shaped by social, cultural, religious or past experiences? Do you view it as a negative thing or as a form of trust in God's design?

_____

_____

_____

_____

_____

_____

_____

_____

_____

_____

_____

REFLECT

How can you better honor your husband's leadership while still expressing your voice and contributions in our marriage?

_____

_____

_____

_____

_____

_____

_____

_____

_____

_____

_____

Guarding Your Marriage: Who Do You Run To?

When conflicts or struggles arise in your marriage, your first instinct might be to turn to friends or family for advice. While seeking counsel isn't inherently wrong, it's crucial to discern where and to whom you run for advice. One of the most dangerous things you can do is to take your marriage problems to people who do not share a biblical view of marriage or who are not equipped to provide godly wisdom.

Single friends, while often well-meaning, may not fully understand the dynamics of a godly marriage. They may unintentionally encourage independence over unity or validate your frustrations in ways that lead you away from reconciliation rather than toward it. For instance, a single friend might suggest that you need more "me time" or that you deserve better if your spouse isn't meeting certain expectations. While personal time is important, the danger comes when advice leads to isolation or an unhealthy view of marriage.

Instead, seek out older, godly couples who have weathered storms in their own marriages. Couples who have a history of faithfulness and perseverance can offer insight that goes beyond surface-level emotions. They understand the deep covenant of marriage and will encourage you to seek God's direction, even in times of conflict.

Another example could be seeking counsel from your pastor or a trusted spiritual mentor who will point you back to God's Word and help you navigate the challenges in a way that strengthens your marriage, rather than fracturing it.

Proverbs 12:15 reminds us that **"the way of fools seems right to them, but the wise listen to advice."** Choose wisely where you seek guidance. When you run to people who understand and value the sanctity of marriage, you safeguard your union against unnecessary damage. Moreover, before running to anyone, your first stop should always be God.

Prayer is not a last resort; it is the foundation of any healthy marriage. Bring your concerns, frustrations, and questions to God, and ask for His wisdom before seeking the counsel of others.

REFLECT

When you face challenges in your marriage, who are the first people you run to for advice? Are they godly mentors who value the covenant of marriage, or do they reflect worldly views?

Final Word on Conflict, Compromise, and Submission

Marriage is not about perfection, but it is about growth—growth as individuals and growth as a couple in Christ. Conflict, compromise, submission, and the wisdom of where to seek counsel are all intertwined in creating a godly marriage that honors both partners and glorifies God. Through every challenge, seek to reflect Christ's humility, patience, and love.

As you prepare for your marriage, keep these principles close. Pray for the strength to handle conflict with grace, the humility to compromise, and the faith to submit, knowing that submission is not a loss of self, but a gain in unity. Above all, guard your marriage by seeking God's guidance and surrounding yourself with those who will uplift you both in times of peace and in times of struggle.

Read the following scriptures and journal your thoughts on how they apply to handling disagreements in a godly way:

- Ephesians 4:2-3 – Be humble, gentle, and patient, striving for unity
- Proverbs 15:1 – A gentle answer turns away wrath
- Colossians 3:13 – Bear with one another and forgive
- James 1:19-20 – Be quick to listen, slow to speak, and slow to anger

How can these verses shape your approach to future conflicts in marriage?

_____

_____

_____

_____

_____

_____

REFLECT

How has seeking advice from single or non-Christian friends impacted your perspective on your relationship? Have they helped enhance your past or current relationships or have they encouraged division or dissatisfaction in some form?

_____

_____

_____

_____

_____

_____

_____

_____

_____

_____

_____

Preparation Prayer

"Lord, I come before You with a heart that desires to honor You in every aspect of my marriage. Teach me to resolve conflict with humility, seeking unity over personal victory. Help me to embrace compromise, not as a loss but as a way to strengthen the bond between my spouse and me. Show me the beauty of submission as You designed it, not as an act of weakness but as an act of trust—trust in You and in the man You've called to lead our family. Guide my steps in seeking counsel, and let me always turn to You first, inviting Your wisdom into every situation. Protect my marriage, Lord, from division, misunderstandings, and worldly influences. Bind us together with love, grace, and understanding as we seek to reflect Your relationship with the Church. In Jesus' name,
Amen

Work Out Your Faith:

Navigating Conflict with Wisdom & Grace

Purpose: To practice handling disagreements in a healthy, biblical, and balanced way while developing skills in compromise, submission, and seeking wise counsel.

Activity: **Role-Playing Healthy Compromise**

- Think of a potential area of disagreement in marriage (e.g., finances, family traditions, career decisions).
- Write out how you would express your perspective with love and respect.
- Now, write how you could also listen, validate your husband's perspective, and find a middle ground.

The Role of Wise Counsel
- Identify two or three godly mentors (e.g., married women you admire, a pastor, or a trusted advisor) whom you can turn to for wisdom in the future.
- Make a commitment to seek counsel when faced with major relational decisions.

CONCLUSION: BECOMING A WIFE PREPARED BY THE KING

As you come to the end of this journey in preparing for your king from the King, remember that the process of becoming a godly wife isn't about perfection —it's about pursuit. You're not striving to check off a list of qualities to "qualify" as a wife, but rather cultivating a heart that seeks to honor God in every aspect of your life and marriage. This journey of preparation is lifelong, one that continues even after you say, "I do."

Marriage is a sacred covenant, a reflection of Christ's love for His Church, and as such, it requires more than just romantic love or shared interests. It demands selflessness, humility, grace, and above all, a foundation built on God's truth. You've explored the importance of conflict resolution, compromise, and submission—not as burdens, but as gifts that strengthen your bond with your husband and deepen your trust in God's design.

The principles we've discussed, from loving like Christ to resolving conflicts with humility, are essential tools for building a marriage that honors God. When challenges arise—and they will—it's your commitment to these godly principles that will allow your relationship to flourish, even in difficult times. Know that your strength as a wife comes not from the world, but from the Holy Spirit who empowers you to love, serve, and support your husband in a way that reflects Christ's love.

As you enter this new season, be mindful of the counsel you keep, the prayers you pray, and the actions you take. Surround yourself with godly influences who encourage you to grow in your role as a wife. Be quick to pray and slow to speak in moments of conflict, seeking peace and understanding before striving for personal victory. Above all, trust that God is your ultimate source of wisdom, comfort, and guidance.

Every step you take in preparation is not just for the future marriage you desire, but for the relationship with God you are cultivating now. As you draw closer to Him, you will become the kind of wife who brings honor to her husband and glory to her King.

Remember, the journey doesn't end here. Continue seeking God daily, and trust Him to shape you into the wife He has called you to be. Your marriage will be a testament not only to the love you share with your husband but also to the faithfulness of the God who brought you together.

Proverbs 31:11-12 "Her husband has full confidence in her and lacks nothing of value. She brings him good, not harm, all the days of her life."

As you prepare for your king, always keep the true King at the center of everything. May your marriage be blessed, rooted in His love, and overflowing with His grace.

REFLECT

How can you allow God's love to flow through you instead of trying to control or manage it yourself? How has your relationship with Christ shaped the kind of partner you desire to be? What characteristics do you want to reflect in your marriage that mirror Christ's love?

REFLECT

What steps can you take today to align your heart with God's will for your life and future marriage? Which topic (e.g. submission, humility) mentioned in this journal do you feel you will have the greatest challenge and how do you plan to prioritize and address it effectively?